SPOTLIGHT ON THE RISE AND FALL OF ANCIENT CIVILIZATIONS™

ANCIENT CHINESE CULTURE

PAULA MORROW

ROSEN
PUBLISHING®
New York

Published in 2017 by The Rosen Publishing Group, Inc.
29 East 21st Street, New York, NY 10010

First Edition

Library of Congress Cataloging-in-Publication Data

Names: Morrow, Paula.
Title: Ancient Chinese culture / Paula Morrow.
Description: First edition. | New York : Rosen Publishing, 2017. | Series: Spotlight on the rise and fall of ancient civilizations | Includes bibliographical references and index. | Audience: Grades 7–12.
Identifiers: LCCN 2016005523| ISBN 9781477788844 (library bound) | ISBN 9781477788820 (pbk.) | ISBN 9781477788837 (6-pack)
Subjects: LCSH: China—Civilization—To 221 B.C.
Classification: LCC DS741.65 .M67 2016 | DDC 931—dc23
LC record available at http://lccn.loc.gov/2016005523

Manufactured in the United States of America

CONTENTS

ANCIENT CHINESE CULTURE

The country of China has close to four thousand years of continuous recorded history. While most ancient civilizations became extinct hundreds or even thousands of years ago, Chinese civilization has endured. This makes China unique in the history of the world. Many of the important arts, philosophies, inventions, and ideals of ancient China are still alive today.

For thousands of years, natural barriers prevented contact with other groups of people: for example, the Gobi Desert in the north and the Himalayan Mountains in the south, deserts and plateaus in the west, and the ocean in the east.

Surrounded by these geographical barriers, the ancient Chinese people believed that their land was the center of a flat earth. One ancient name for China is Zhongguo, which means "Middle Kingdom" or "Center of the World." This name is still a common name for China today.

Cut off from contact with the outside world by mountains, deserts, and the Pacific Ocean, China developed its own unique civilization.

THE YELLOW RIVER

The Yellow River is the world's muddiest river. Stretching across China for more than three thousand miles (4,828 kilometers), it flows from central Asia to the Pacific Ocean. The water travels through areas where the soil is easily eroded, picking up silt and carrying it downstream. This silt constantly replenishes the land of the river valley, nourishing a fertile plain well suited to agriculture. The silt sometimes fills the riverbed and blocks the water's flow, causing widespread floods. Flooding has caused the river to change course more than twenty times.

The Yellow River is called the cradle of Chinese civilization. Recent archaeological discoveries show that Chinese civilization actually developed in many areas before it merged into a single culture. Nevertheless, the river holds a special status in the history of China.

The river may be a symbol of the Chinese spirit. It bears burdens (the silt), it adapts (its course changes), and it endures (it continues to flow).

The Mother River Monument in the city of Lanzhou symbolizes the Yellow River as a nurturing mother caring for the land and people of China.

SHANG DYNASTY

For thousands of years, people thought the Shang dynasty was a myth or legend. In 1928, scientists discovered the ancient city of Anyang in the Yellow River Valley. Anyang was a large city untouched since ancient times. Its discovery can be called the beginning of modern archaeology in China.

The rich and magnificent tombs at Anyang hid something more valuable than gold or jewels. They held writing, the oldest written records in China.

Most of the records were written not on scrolls or clay tablets but on metal or bone. Pictograms, simple pictures that represented words, were inscribed on flat bones or turtle shells. These were called oracle bones because they were used to tell fortunes. Bronze objects such as pots and cups also had pictograms on them. The early pictograms were the first form of writing in China. Over time, they have developed into the characters of modern Chinese writing.

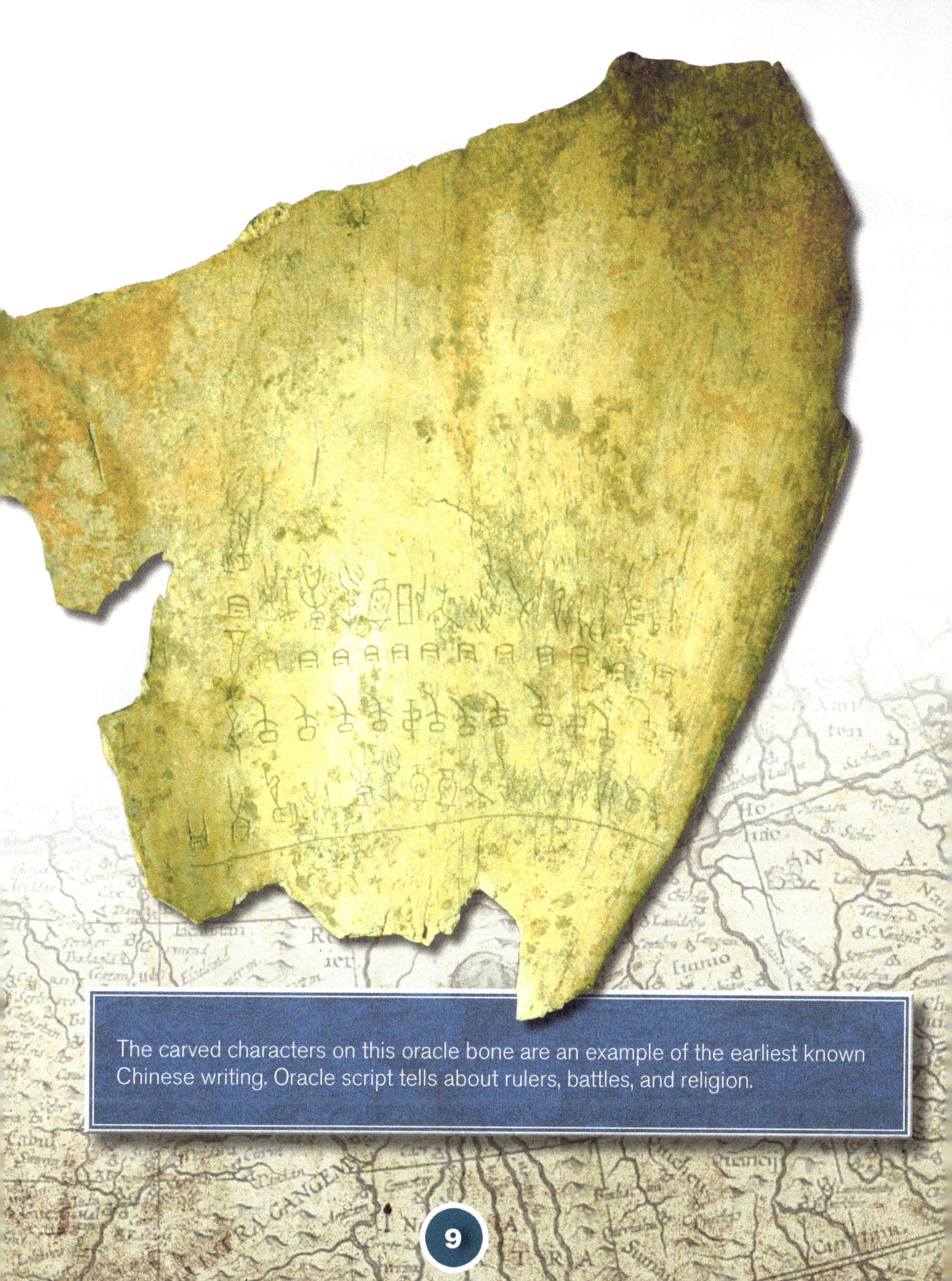

The carved characters on this oracle bone are an example of the earliest known Chinese writing. Oracle script tells about rulers, battles, and religion.

BRONZE IN EARLY CHINA

Every archaeological site from the Shang dynasty onward contains hundreds and even thousands of bronze artifacts. Bronze, which is an alloy of copper and tin, can be cast into durable and beautiful objects. Many of the bronze artifacts were cast with inscriptions telling about people and events.

Bronze dishes, pots, and cauldrons were used for cooking and storing food. Even simple everyday vessels were decorated with geometric patterns, stylized animals, or Chinese characters.

Ritual bronze vessels were used for both ceremonies and sacrifices. Often they were decorated with a monster figure that is not found on any other bronze objects.

When the king wanted to honor someone, he would give that person a bronze vessel with an inscription describing the person's deeds. This became a family treasure, handed down from generation to generation. The inscriptions on these special vessels help modern archaeologists understand ancient Chinese culture.

A bronze vessel from the Shang dynasty shows a stylized *chaj-cha* bird. This vessel was used for ceremonial purposes in the thirteenth century BCE.

FIRST WRITING

Bronze inscriptions detailed the exploits of heroes on earth. But oracle bone inscriptions found in Shang tombs were a form of communication with ancestors in heaven.

The first oracle bones were scapulas, or shoulder blades, of oxen or deer, which are flat and smooth. Later the scribes and kings preferred tortoise or turtle shells, usually the shell's flat bottom.

Next, Chinese characters were painted on the fabric with a brush. Archaeologists have found pieces of silk from the Warring States period showing calligraphy.

Around the fifth century BCE, Chinese scribes began writing on wooden tablets and bamboo. Bamboo was sliced into strips, tied together with string, and formed into a roll. These strips hold the earliest manuscripts of classical Chinese literature, such as the works of Laozi and Confucius.

Oracle bones script is the first known form of Chinese writing. This writing has evolved and expanded. The beautiful calligraphy still used today is directly related to these early scripts.

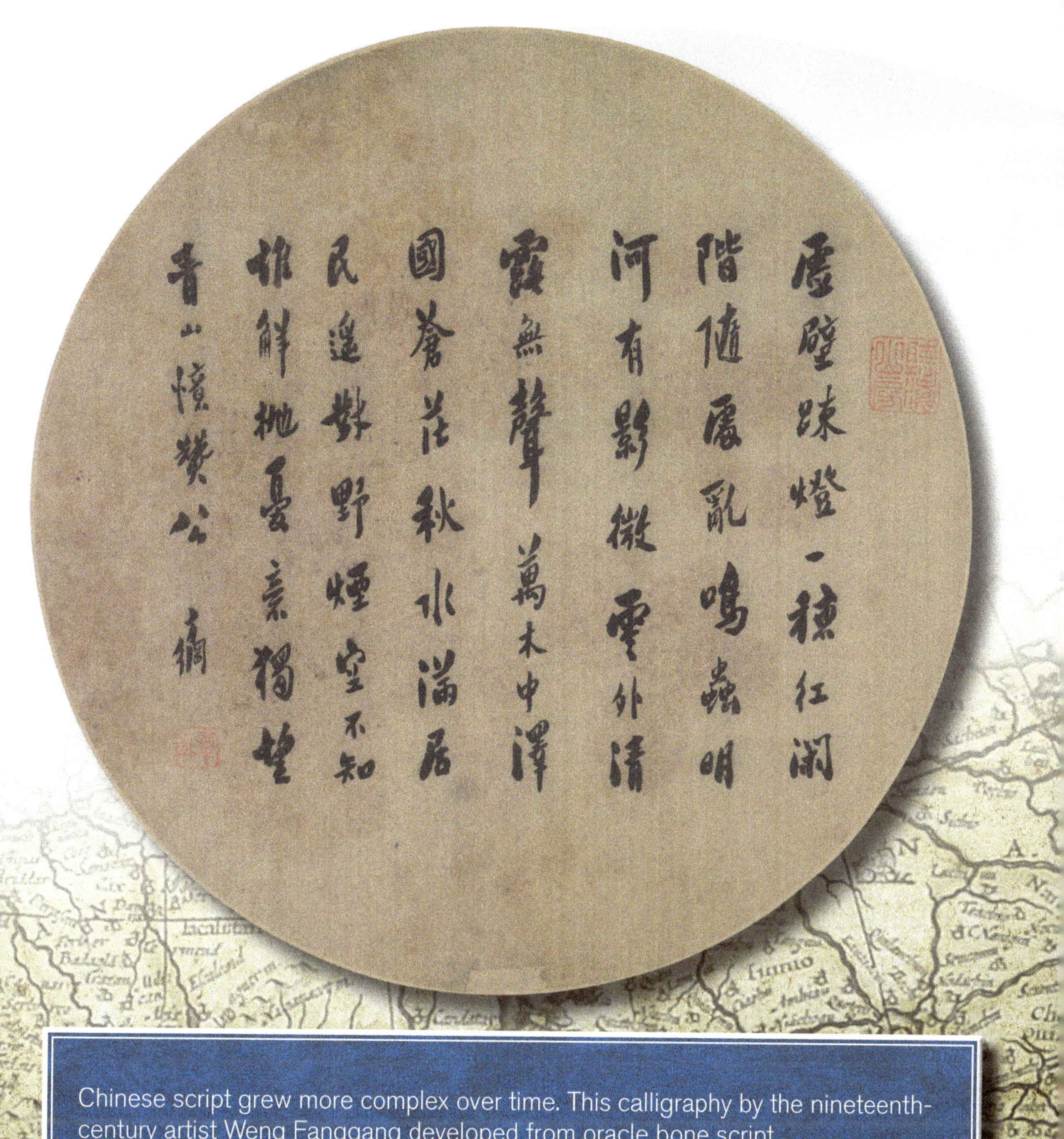

Chinese script grew more complex over time. This calligraphy by the nineteenth-century artist Weng Fanggang developed from oracle bone script.

ZHOU DYNASTY

The Zhou dynasty was the longest-lasting dynasty in the history of China. This dynasty held power for eight hundred years. When Zhou Wu, the king of the Zhou tribe, attacked and overthrew the last Shang king, he claimed he had a "Mandate of Heaven" to rule. This began a period of great progress but also of harsh government control.

As Zhou territory grew and expanded, it split into many smaller states. During the Spring and Autumn period, these states varied by tribe and culture, as well as philosophy, religion, and even language. Many scholars taught their own ideas, resulting in so many that it was eventually called the time of "One Hundred Schools of Thought."

The squabbles between the many states led to the Warring States period. Military might and more advanced weapons became a priority. By the end of this period, only eight kingdoms remained.

A portrait of Zhou dynasty Emperor Wu Ti shows majesty and dignity. It was painted by the seventh-century artist Yen Li-pen in his *Scroll of the Emperors.*

MILITARY MIGHT

By the Zhou dynasty, iron weapons and tools had become common in China. Iron is forged rather than cast and has a higher melting point than bronze. Troops armed with iron had a great advantage over tribes with bronze weapons.

Large armies might have one thousand chariots and twenty thousand foot soldiers. Over time, armies stopped using chariots, which were more difficult to drive over hills and uneven ground. Nobles were mounted on horseback, accompanied by hundreds of thousands of lower-class infantrymen, or soldiers who fought on foot.

The general Sun Tzu (who called himself Sun Wu) wrote a book called *The Art of War* during the Zhou dynasty. This classic text on military strategy and tactics had a great influence from ancient times until the present. It stresses understanding one's enemy and if possible winning without fighting. Sun Tzu wrote that one should first try strategy and diplomacy before going into battle.

During the Warring States period, rulers of different states had bronze spear-heads decorated with special patterns. This example, with curved cutting edges, is from the state of Yue.

CHINESE PHILOSOPHY

While the Warring States period was a time of political and social turmoil, it was also a time when philosophy flourished. With no central authority in control, scholars and former noblemen were free to teach and write their own ideas. Many of them became itinerant philosophers, taking their ideas from village to town, or gathered groups of disciples around themselves. Across the separate states, scholars discussed and debated hundreds of concepts in "One Hundred Schools of Thought."

Two great philosophers arose during this period. These were men whose ideas have survived for more than two thousand years. They were Confucius, for whom Confucianism is named, and Laozi, the founder of Daoism.

Many other religious and philosophical schools existed, too, but their thoughts were not passed on to later generations. When the Qin emperor Shi Huang came into power, he burned any writings with which he did not agree.

The influence of Confucius has lasted for 2500 years and is still strong in China today. This statue of Confucius stands in Nanjing.

QIN DYNASTY

The Qin dynasty is memorable as a time of both consolidation and expansion. The governor of the state of Qin defeated the Zhou king and made himself emperor. A harsh ruler, Qin Shi Huang and the leaders in his court introduced a strict philosophy called legalism. They forced everyone to agree with them.

Qin Shi Huang standardized measures that had been different in the different states, such as weights, coins, laws, and writing. He burned books with which he did not agree. Out of the "One Hundred Schools of Thought," he allowed only books by Confucius, classics, and a few texts on history, medicine, astronomy, and agriculture.

He forced thousands of slaves and prisoners to work on major projects, such as the Dujiangyan irrigation project, Qin mausoleum, and famous Great Wall of China. His mausoleum, or tomb, and the irrigation project were started while he was governor of Qin and completed after he became emperor.

The Dujiangyan irrigation system was built by filling bamboo baskets with stones for barriers to change the course of the Minjiang River. Today's system irrigates over 5,300 square kilometers (2,046 square miles) of land.

BUILDINGS AND ARCHITECTURE

The earliest Chinese architecture tended to be wood or earthen structures, perhaps because of a lack of available stone building materials. Walls and foundations of houses and other buildings were commonly made of rammed earth. Damp clay, sand, and gravel were combined and packed into a framework. This packed wall hardened into a strong and durable structure. Buildings also used timber. Columns rather than the walls supported the roof's weight.

Only walls and tombs remain of most buildings from before the Han period, but the ancient Chinese created small models of houses, barns, and other structures. These were placed in tombs for the dead, which they were believed to need in the afterlife. Architecture was also described in written records. One Han palace may have been surrounded by tall towers of timber, stone, and brick. Walls inside important buildings were covered with paintings of historical scenes and portraits. Architects were highly honored by the emperors.

The columns inside this Han dynasty tomb have supported the roof for more than two thousand years. The walls are decorated with stylized figures.

TOMBS AND FUNERAL CUSTOMS

Royal or noble persons were buried with everything they would need for a future life after death. Their tombs were furnished with household items, personal objects, weapons, and religious vessels. In addition, the tombs of royalty and nobility included furniture, as well as chariots and horses for the person's afterlife.

Often objects made of a stone called jade were buried with the body, because jade was believed to prevent decay and symbolize immortality. Ferocious or mythical animals made of clay or bronze guarded the tomb against evil spirits. Tigers and dragons were popular guardians.

During the early dynasties, servants and slaves were buried in the tombs to serve the person in the afterlife. The tombs at Anyang contained hundreds of victims. In later periods, models of servants were buried instead of living slaves.

A vast army of life-size warriors made of terracotta guarded the great tomb of Emperor Qin Shi Huang.

A vast army of individual, life-size warriors guarded the tomb of Emperor Qin Shi Huang. The face on each statue was different from every other face.

HAN DYNASTY

The Han dynasty lasted for four centuries. This time of stability and prosperity has been called one of the golden ages of Chinese history. The Han copied the Qin pattern of centralized government, but legalism was combined with Confucian ideals of virtue and moderation. Thus the economy expanded, territory increased almost to the size of present-day China, and culture blossomed.

Trade developed along the routes called the Silk Road, and the Han exchanged ideas and technologies with the outside world. Emperor Wudi (Wu the Great) started a Confucian academy. Anyone applying for a government job had to pass a test showing his qualifications. Mathematical texts from the Han period show arithmetic, algebra, and geometry.

Confucianism, Daoism, and the newer Buddhism flourished alongside earlier native regional beliefs. Daoism developed into China's major religion and is still practiced today.

This dynasty established what became known as Chinese culture so well that "Han" became the term for someone who is Chinese.

Emperor Wudi, the seventh emperor of the Western Han Dynasty, was also an outstanding statesman, military strategist, and poet.

SILK ROAD

Silk was first discovered in China in prehistoric times. Early bone inscriptions mention silkworms and mulberry trees, showing that silk was common before written language. It was essential in the daily life of all social classes, used as clothing, wrapping material, decoration, and art. Silk making was a thriving industry during the Zhou dynasty.

For millennia, silk was unknown in other parts of the world. After Alexander the Great tried to invade India, some descendants of his army wandered into China. Emperor Wudi sent a representative westward to meet the outsiders in 138 BCE. Soon trading began, and silk became a highly prized luxury in Rome and throughout the Mediterranean lands.

The Silk Road was a series of trade routes by land and by sea. Although silk was the major trade item from China, cultural exchanges also thrived. China, India, Persia, Arabia, and Europe shared goods, technologies, literature, philosophies, religions, and more.

Mulberry leaves are the only food silkworms eat. This nineteenth-century painting shows a woman picking leaves to feed silkworms.

LITERATURE

The invention of paper changed the world. Around 105, Cai Lun had the idea of making sheets of paper from plant fiber. The emperor honored him for his invention, which spread across China and beyond.

Writings on bone or bronze had been limited to historical, business, and religious texts. Paper made other forms of literature possible. The earliest poetry developed from work songs, prayers, and love songs. Myths and legends were told as oral poems. Confucius edited the first written collection of poems, *Classic of Poetry* (*Shijing*).

The Han imperial library included works on philosophy, religion, the arts, mathematics, science, and medicine. Street performers told stories in ancient China, which were later written down and developed into novels.

Paper allowed scholars to copy rare silk and bamboo books from earlier periods to reach more readers. While it is unknown how much literature was destroyed in Emperor Qin's book burning, the remaining texts make up China's classic literature.

Paper was made by boiling and beating bark, hemp, rags, and old fishnets to a pulp. This paste was spread in very thin sheets and dried into paper.

POTTERY

Early pottery was made by shaping a paste of clay, quartz, and feldspar. These shapes were baked in special ovens called kilns. The high temperature made them hard enough to use as pots, cups, and so on. Potters carved designs and pictures on the clay shapes before baking them. Glazing the pots made them smooth and shiny. Sometimes the glazes were in many colors.

Porcelain is finer and harder than clay pottery. It is also more waterproof and airtight. Porcelain must be baked, or "fired," at higher temperatures, making it stronger. High heat is also needed to cast bronze, so developing better kilns may have helped the Chinese discover how to work with bronze. The earliest known porcelain is from the Shang dynasty.

Next came lustrous vessels called greenware in China and celadon in the West. This pottery was widespread early in the Western Han dynasty and beyond.

The distinctive greenish tones of celadon occur when clay rich in iron oxide is fired in a kiln with minimal oxygen. This vase is from the first century CE.

PAINTING

The Chinese were using pictures to express their imaginations before written history began. They painted on pottery in the Stone Age. Ancient rock drawings have been found in the Red Mountains. However, painting as an art form in itself developed later.

Painting and calligraphy are very closely related, because Chinese characters began as pictograms. Like calligraphy, traditional Chinese painting involves using long-haired brushes, ink, and watercolor on silk or paper.

The earliest paintings that still exist are from the Zhou period. One shows a woman with a phoenix and a dragon, the other a man with the same creatures. Both are painted on silk.

Paintings of the Han dynasty use simple lines to express ideas. Figure painting focuses on human beings. Landscape painting emphasizes the relationship between humans and nature. These paintings were sometimes on rolls of silk, and other times they were created on standing room-divider screens.

Few paintings from early times have survived. This twelfth-century painting shows the influence of ink lines of earlier works.

MUSIC

The earliest musical instruments recorded in the Shang period were bells and drums. Chime stones and bronze chime bells were hung on racks according to size. Musicians played elegant, tuned rhythms on them during rituals and ceremonies.

During the Qin and Han dynasties, music for song and dance became popular. An Imperial Music Bureau collected folk songs, composed new works, and performed. Pipes and stringed instruments provided fast and strong rhythms. The Han dynasty also included ethnic instruments from different parts of China.

The largest store of musical instruments ever found in China was the tomb of a nobleman in Suzhou. It contained zithers, flutes, panpipes, drums, and chime stones. Most amazing was a set of sixty-four cast bronze bells, which weighs about three tons. The tomb included two music rooms; one held the bronze bells and chime stones used for somber ritual music, the other held instruments for entertainment. These were used for banquets, folk music, and accompanying singers and dancers.

Statues of musicians were sometimes placed in tombs to entertain the person in the afterlife. This pair of clay figurines dates from the Han dynasty.

DANCE

Confucius taught that poems express people's feelings, songs express people's hopes, and dance moves people by images. All three art forms began in ritual. Religious dance was a form of communicating with the gods and ancestors.

During the Shang dynasty, dance was an important part of worship and prayer. The Shang also had courtly dances that were entertainment rather than ritual.

Dance was a form of education in the Zhou dynasty. Dancers acted out the feats of kings and ancestors. Later, these heroic dances developed into an early form of drama. Formal theater and Chinese opera did not begin until after the Han period.

The Han dynasty continued the tradition of having two kinds of dance. Ritual dance was formal or martial and was performed by men. Dances to entertain featured female dancers and were more graceful in style. In addition to the two formal kinds of dances, there were informal, private dances.

Performers twirl joss sticks in the Fire Dragon Dance during the Moon Festival in modern-day Hong Kong. This popular celebration dates back to the Zhou dynasty.

WHAT REMAINS TODAY

China is unique in the history of the world because it is the only civilization that has survived from ancient times until now. Many of the important arts, philosophies, inventions, and ideals of ancient China have spread around the world and are still alive today.

Among the many inventions from ancient China that are still in use are paper, printing, gunpowder, the compass, the seismograph, and silk. Tea was first discovered in China. Herbal medicines, acupuncture, and massage all began in China, as did martial arts.

Confucianism and Daoism have many living followers, and *The Art of War* is applied in modern situations. China was the first country to test applicants for civil service jobs.

Calligraphy remains an important art form, and modern Chinese characters are similar to those used in the ancient world. The Dujiangyan irrigation system built in 256 BCE waters farmland today, and the Great Wall of China still marches across the land.

The Great Wall displays the highly developed architecture, technology, and art of ancient China. Today it remains the national symbol for safeguarding the country and its people.

alloy A metal made by mixing together two naturally occurring metals.

ancestor A family member one is descended from, such as a grandparent or great-grandparent.

artifact An object made by hand, especially one from an earlier time.

calligraphy The art of writing beautifully, or a highly decorative handwriting.

cast To shape or form in a mold.

dynasty A series of rulers who come from the same family.

exploit A great deed, feat, or accomplishment.

fertile Able to produce crops, vegetation, and other growth.

forge Made by being heated and then hammered into shape while still hot.

itinerant Traveling from place to place, especially along a regular route, or working in one place for a short time, then moving to another place for work.

kiln An oven for baking or drying something, especially one for firing pottery or baking bricks.

mandate A command, order, decree, or law.

oracle A divine communication or revelation, or a person who delivers such a communication.

philosophy A system of thinking about truth, knowledge, and life.

pictogram A sign or symbol such as a drawing that represents a word.

replenish To fill again.

silt Fine sand or earthy material that is carried by running water and settles to the bottom of a channel.

terracotta A hard, reddish-brown unglazed earthenware.

The Art Institute of Chicago
111 South Michigan Avenue
Chicago, IL 60603
(312) 443-3600
Website: artic.edu
The Art Institute's distinguished Asian collection contains works spanning nearly five millennia. It includes Chinese bronzes, ceramics, jades, and textiles. The museum's Ryerson & Burnham Libraries is one of the finest U.S. research libraries for art and architecture.

The British Museum
Great Russell Street
London, WC1B 3DG
England
+44 (0)20 7323 8299
The British Museum's special Chinese exhibits include the Joseph E. Hotung Gallery, Chinese jade in the Selwyn and Ellie Alleyne Gallery, and Chinese ceramics in the Sir Joseph Hotung Centre for Ceramic Studies.

Embassy of the People's Republic of China in the United States of America
3505 International Place NW
Washington, DC 20008
(202) 495-2266
Website: china-embassy.org
The Embassy of China serves as a liaison between the United States and China. It also disseminates cultural, educational, and historical information about China.

The Field Museum
1400 S. Lake Shore Drive
Chicago, IL 60605
(312) 922-9410
Website: www.feldmuseum.org
The Cyrus Tang Hall of China, a permanent exhibition at the Field
    Museum, covers thousands of years of history, and showcases tex-
    tiles, rubbings, bronzes, ceramics, and sculpture.

The Smithsonian Institution
Freer Gallery of Art
Jefferson Drive at 12th Street SW
and
Arthur M. Sackler Gallery
1050 Independence Avenue SW
Washington, DC 20013
(202) 633-7012
The Smithsonian Institution has two museums of Asian art: the Freer
    Gallery of Art and the Arthur M. Sackler Gallery. The Smithsonian
    has more than ten thousand objects including nearly every medi-
    um and category of Chinese art.

WEBSITES

Because of the changing nature of Internet links, Rosen Publishing has developed an online list of websites related to the subject of this book. This site is
updated regularly. Please use this link to access the list:

http://www.rosenlinks.com/SRFAC/ccult

Bramwell, Neil D. *Discover Ancient China* (Discover Ancient Civilizations). Berkeley Heights, NJ: Enslow, 2014.

Collins, Terry. *Ancient China* (You Choose: Historical Eras). North Mankato, MN: Capstone, 2012.

Holm, Kirsten. *Everyday Life in Ancient China* (Jr. Graphic Ancient Civilizations). New York, NY: Powerkids Press, 2012.

Kramer, Lance. *Great Ancient China Projects: 25 Great Projects You Can Build Yourself*. White River Junction, VT: Nomad Press, 2014.

Liu-Perkins, Christine, and Sarah S. Brannen. *At Home in Her Tomb: Lady Dai and the Ancient Chinese Treasures of Mawangdui*. Watertown, MA: Charlesbridge, 2014.

Nagle, Jeanne. *Discovering Ancient China* (Exploring Ancient Civilizations). New York, NY: Rosen Publishing, 2015.

Ransom, Candice. *Tools and Treasures of Ancient China* (Searchlight Books). Minneapolis, MN: Lerner Publications, 2014.

Roberts, Russ. *Ancient China* (Explore Ancient Worlds). Hockessin, DE: Mitchell Lane, 2012.

Rosinsky, Natalie M. *Ancient China*. (Exploring the Ancient World). North Mankato, MN: Compass Point, 2012.

Sen, Benita. *Smart Green Civilizations: Ancient China*. New Delhi, India: The Energy and Resources Institute, 2015.

Steele, Philip. *Hands-On History! Ancient China: Step into the Time of the Chinese Empire, with 15 step-by-step Projects*. Leicestershire, England: Armadillo, 2013.

Tsiang, Sarah, and Martha Newbigging. *Warriors and Wailers: One Hundred Ancient Chinese Jobs You Might Have Relished or Reviled*. Toronto, ON, Canada: Annick, 2012.

BIBLIOGRAPHY

Dan, Yao et al. *Chinese Literature: Great Tradition Since The Book of Songs.* Translated by Li Ziliang et al. Beijing, China: Intercontinental Press, 2010.

Hays, Jeffrey. "Themes in Chinese History." Facts and Details, June 2015. Retrieved December 10, 2015 (http://factsanddetails.com/china/cat2/sub1/item31.html).

Liu, Li. *The Archaeology of China: From the Late Paleolithic to the Early Bronze Age.* Cambridge: Cambridge University Press, 2012.

Pearlstein, Elinor L. and James T. Ulak. *Asian Art in The Art Institute of Chicago.* Chicago, IL: The Institute, 1993.

Schuster, Angela M. H. "At the Museums: Ancient Chinese Treasures." Archaeology, Vol. 53 no. 3, May/June 2000. Retrieved March 21, 2016 (http://archive.archaeology.org/0005/etc/museum1.html).

"Silk Artistry of the Qin, Han, Wei, and Jin Dynasties." *Chinese Silks,* ed. by Kuh, Dieter. New Haven, CT: Yale University Press, 2012.

Tzu, Sun. *The Art of War,* translated by Lionel Giles. Internet Classics Archive. Retrieved December 17, 2015 (http://classics.mit.edu/Tzu/artwar.html).

Watson, William. *China Before the Han Dynasty.* New York, NY: F. Praeger, 1961.

Yong, Jin. *Arts in China.* Translated by Wang Pingxing and Zhao Xiufu. Beijing, China: China Intercontinental Press, 2007.

Zhiyan, Li, and Cheng Wen. "Pottery from the Shang and Zhou to the Qin and Han Dynasties." *Chinese Pottery and Porcelain.* Beijing, China: Foreign Languages Press, 1989.

INDEX

ABOUT THE AUTHOR

Paula Morrow has been fascinated by oriental art and culture ever since she was a child and her grandparents told her stories about the Chinese antiques in their home. A professional librarian, she became immersed in the research for this book. Morrow is a former executive editor at Cricket Magazine Group. She is the author of a number of nonfiction books and e-books for various publishers.

PHOTO CREDITS